An **Introduction** *To* **Entrepreneurship**

Don't Sink The Ship

Anthony Robinson

Copyright © 2021 Anthony Robinson. All rights reserved.

No part of this report may be modified or altered in any form whatsoever, electronic, or mechanical, including photocopying, recording, or by any informational storage or retrieval system without express written, dated, and signed permission from the author.

TABLE OF CONTENT

An Introduction To Entrepreneurship 4

Entrepreneurship Mindset 6

Launching A Business 14

Pros And Cons To Hiring Family Members 18

Don't Celebrate Without Paying Taxes 24

Importance Of A Good Cpa 25

Learn To Outsource Or To Delegate Workloads, You Can't Do It Alone 34

How To Outsource And Delegate Specific Tasks Within Your Company 37

Duplicate And Scale-Up 39

Pay Yourself 45

Keep Personal Accounts And Business Accounts Separate 49

Don't Allow Your Good Heart To Create Bad Business Decisions 56

An Introduction To Entrepreneurship

This book is an introduction to entrepreneurship, and its approach is resolutely interdisciplinary. Its objective is to present to the reader the different aspects of the entrepreneurial process and demystify it. At the end of its reading, students will have acquired and developed the tools of analysis and reflection to understand the importance of entrepreneurship and its processes. It is divided into five main parts: the framework, the approach, the methods, and the evolution of the activity and, finally, the different facets of entrepreneurship.

It is aimed at an audience of students in the human sciences, exact and applied, and anyone wishing to understand entrepreneurship better. It has been designed for diverse audiences and does not require any prerequisites.

Entrepreneurship is seen as a means to improve a country's competitiveness, foster economic growth, and increase employment opportunities. Researchers and decision-makers agree that an entrepreneurial economy is a dynamic and innovative economy that is to say who experiment with new ideas, new products, or processes, which allow it to renew itself.

Entrepreneurship is tough to define. More specifically, the concept of entrepreneurship considers the impact on the environment and the influence of this environment to arouse business development by providing more or less vital resources and conventions.

We can define entrepreneurship as "the action human," supported by the surrounding environment, to generate value in the market through creation or the development of the economic activity, evolving with this value and ultimately affecting the economy, to better respond to individual and collective needs of territory there are a large number of definitions of entrepreneurship, but some key dimensions can be retained. We can include the following sizes, i.e., the creation of a new company or own employment; the creation of new products or processes; taking so much risk for the entrepreneur than for the company; innovation, whatever the form; the outcome of value; the company's ability to generate profits and grow, locating and exploiting one or more several business opportunities and the mobilization of resources, whether limited or not.

Entrepreneurship is a significant engine of economic and social development. That is why it is essential to make young people aware of it, to consider launching a new activity that creates value.

More generally, an entrepreneurial mindset can be useful inside or outside any organization - public or private, profit-oriented or not - and our society, as a whole, needs individuals with the right skills.

Entrepreneurship Mindset

The Entrepreneurial Mindset refers to the dispositions of mind, a specific way of thinking, and a set of attitudes, which drive entrepreneurs and maintain them within a particular framework of action, Entrepreneurial Action.

A list of ten attributes of the Entrepreneurial Mindset should allow you to develop this mindset effectively. Décor related to its economic and commercial considerations, the entrepreneurial state of mind can be born or reborn among the school fact actors.

The Attributes Of The Entrepreneurial Mindset

Multiple items can call a state of mind (Mindset): skills, attitudes, habits, postures, perceptions, beliefs, experiences, beliefs, skills, knowledge, traits, virtues, or particular logic. The entrepreneurial mindset is not made up of the technical skills necessary for the entrepreneurial profession's exercise.

The Entrepreneurial Mindset is made up of personal and social skills. They are manifested in entrepreneurs' capacity to find success in their businesses, independently and sometimes despite an unfavorable external context.

These skills are not the subject of a single description. There are many lists. Despite this, a narrow list of ten attributes suffices to characterize the entrepreneurial mindset on an operational level. In practice, the knowledge, awareness, understanding, and development of these ten attributes represent the framework to be considered to support entrepreneurs in an entrepreneurial mindset coaching system effectively.

THESE NINE ATTRIBUTES ARE:

- Creativity
- Curiosity
- Association: capacity to consolidate, to see openings, essential reasoning Initiative, and autonomy
- Ability to solve problems
- Ability to create value
- Ability to work with available resources
- Ability to make decisions that take into account constraints
- "Timely achiever": the ability to engage and disengage, persistence/resilience
- Promoter and builder of relationships

What exactly is the entrepreneurial mindset?

Man is a creative being. The entrepreneur knows how to use his creativity to put it at the service of a vision, a personal objective, or a cause. He mobilizes his skills for this: knowledge, know-how, interpersonal skills, communication skills, interpersonal and social expertise, personality traits, attitudes, etc.

Here are the main traits that characterize the entrepreneurial mindset.

1. **Accept the impermanence of things.**

    Uncertainty and the impermanence of things do not make the entrepreneur anxious. Instead, he realizes what they can offer as opportunities.

2. **Agree to adapt.**

    Adaptability is a critical point in an entrepreneurial process. Entrepreneurial life is set apart by the standard urge appearance of new difficulties. The business visionary consents to address himself to adjust to the market. It looks to grow new upper hands.

3. **Have a vision.**

    This aspect of the entrepreneurial mindset touches on inspiration. Vision is the sine qua non-condition to unite around the project. The entrepreneurial vision makes it possible to set coherent, clear, and stable objectives. It makes it possible to draw a common thread for each of the actions to be taken to succeed in your business. Correlated to the manager's will, it must evolve to develop beyond the current market limits.

Having an entrepreneurial vision means inventing tomorrow and anticipating what the world could be like in a few years.

4. **Be optimistic.**

   Optimism characterizes the entrepreneurial state of mind because it allows to rationally identify the causes of failure, to bounce back from a loss, to gain perspectives.

5. **Be motivated.**

   What would starting a business be without motivation? Motivation is the engine that moves the mountains of obstacles that stand on the entrepreneurial path. It is this thing that will not give up. It is also what will make it possible to redouble our efforts when new opportunities arise. Motivation can be fueled by different kinds of fuel: money, values, and beliefs.

6. **Have a good dose of resilience.**

   Resilience is the ability to recover after an error, failure, or accident. It allows you to bounce back after a hard blow; it is worked by letting go.

7. **Possess a faculty of synergy.**

   To create a business is to be part of an ecosystem, you don't do it alone. The company is part of a dynamic environment, often wealthy, sometimes hostile, but essential to its survival. The business manager must become aware of the importance of the network and the relationship to fit this environment best.

Five Tips For Consolidating Your Entrepreneurial Spirit:

- » Broaden your horizon (think wide)
- » Make the best of your business plan
- » Discover and cultivate your competitive advantages,
- » Increase your involvement by choosing an idea that matches who you are.
- » Define what success means to you.

The four pillars of the entrepreneurial spirit: the character of the entrepreneur An entrepreneur is a person who creates a project from a vision and resources in his possession. If each entrepreneur is different because of his history, experiences, values, and vision, they all have the same state of mind: the entrepreneurial spirit. Why is it so important, and what can it be done? How is this state of mind characterized? Who can adopt and cultivate this mindset?

Entrepreneurial spirit: the key to a successful entrepreneurial adventure When we think of entrepreneurship in USA, we too often think of "startup." What is a startup? Unfortunately, for many entrepreneurs, this term usually means the following:

- » I have a decided undertaking, yet I need an enormous heap of cash to make it. I will subsequently search for resources from:"
- » -Banks (and therefore get into debt)
- » Investors (and therefore gradually lose control of the capital and therefore of my company)
- » Crowdfunding (but in the end it doesn't work that easily)

This money will allow me to develop the box for three years and to hold out because I will lose a lot of money (I will not have any customers during this launch phase). After five years, I will have managed to reach the critical size to sell it and make a nice profit (if I manage to survive by then). "

The problem with this vision is that the entrepreneur does not control the process: he relies on external resources to build a project, to the detriment of the available resources. From my extended research and my personal experience, I realized that successful entrepreneurial adventures were based mainly on the internal resources of entrepreneurs (their soft skills) and, in particular, four essential pillars:

» Vision
» Motivation
» Resilience
» Login

The vision pillar: The basis of entrepreneurship that is the pillar that allows you to set a clear goal and guide your choices and actions towards this goal. This vision also will enable you to be creative and find new ways of innovating. The entrepreneur's dream is based in part on his intuition and intention.

This vision pillar is a real muscle that can be trained and developed. Think of those visionary entrepreneurs who exercised their minds just to succeed in visualizing beyond what was visible in their market. Your customers may know what they want, but may not be aware of their real needs. It is up to the entrepreneur to be visionary enough to understand his client's requirements fully; the entrepreneur is a specialist in conditions.

The Motivation pillar: The very essence of action you've probably noticed it, but entrepreneurs are generally very motivated people. Even if they face big problems or challenges, they still have the enthusiasm and energy to move forward. It is this motivation that enables them to act.

Motivation is a real fuel for action: by understanding the meaning of what we are doing and the objective's interest to be achieved, even if the task is painful, we will achieve it. Conversely, when you are not motivated, it becomes much more difficult to act.

The entrepreneur, being a person of actions, must at all costs maintain his motivation. The good news is that basis is also a soft skill, a muscle that trains through reflexes and exercises.

The Resilience pillar: keep moving forward despite the difficulties, Are you an entrepreneur? I'm sure you spend more time dealing with contingencies and problems than creating business plans! Hence the importance of working on your resilience: your ability to "take" a problem and bounce back. An entrepreneur knows how to adapt, and that is what makes his strength.

Here again, just like vision and motivation, resilience is a soft skill that develops with will and time.

The Connection pillar: knowing how to surround yourself to better advance

I am convinced that co-creating (making synergies) is much more powerful than creating alone. Alone we speed up, and together we go further. One of the reflexes of entrepreneurs is always to see what connections they can create, either for their project or to help others.

An entrepreneur is a connector; he connects people who will positively impact him and his business. Through his ability to communicate, systemic thinking, and empathy, he will create synergies. This pillar is also a skill that is developing and which is indispensable for entrepreneurs.

Entrepreneurial spirit: it's not just for business creators, of course, the entrepreneurial spirit and its four pillars are essential for a creator and entrepreneur. Be that as it may, it isn't held distinctly for this populace. Company employees can also be enterprising and cultivate this same state of mind!

Launching A Business

Starting a business: 10 tips to get started.

1. **Ask yourself what are your qualities and shortcomings**

   "Right when you start a business, you have to proceed in stages unquestionably the main thing is to do a personal evaluation.

   What are my real motivations? What are my strengths and weaknesses? Do I have the necessary diplomas and know-how? Am I a good salesperson? Will I be able to convince? Am I a good manager? A good technician?

   Once this analysis has been carried out, if you have detected any shortcomings, you must ask yourself how to remedy them.

2. **Evaluate your financial situation carefully**

   Before you leave on the formation of a business, study your monetary circumstance well. You probably will not be able to pay yourself the first year of production. On the off chance that you live with your folks, it is ideal to remain there somewhat more!

On the off chance that you are in work, you have the opportunity of mentioning low maintenance work for setting up a business. That can be an answer to keep part of your compensation. On the off chance that you have no pay and nobody can have you, do you have reserve funds that will permit you to meet the first fixed costs of the business?

3. **Find associates**

"Young entrepreneurs often create a project with others. And they're right, and it's a formula that works. The complementarity of aptitudes is a significant resource when setting up a business. Notwithstanding, before you start, ask yourself the correct inquiries: do all of you have a similar vision for the organization? Are you in phase with its future development? What place does everyone want there to be? Who makes what decision? What is the level of responsibility as expected and cash of each? Etc." Create a business with one or more partners.

4. **Discussion about your business creation venture around you**

"Make an effort not to start alone without having faced your endeavor with experienced people. Ability to hear them out and question yourself. A business chief must have an incredible capacity to adjust. "

5. **Create a business: get support**

It is essential not to be left alone and to get help from the start of your project. Get in touch with support organizations such as chambers of commerce and industry

(CCI), sections of trades and crafts, management shops, or even specific youth networks, which offer a tutoring system between young designers and experienced entrepreneurs. Most are free or paid for by available help instruments.

You can likewise attempt to get into a hatchery or an action and work helpful (CAE). These structures permit you to test your life-size venture without facing any challenges. They exist all over USA.

Finally, if you are in contact with entrepreneurs, ask them for advice. There is great solidarity in the community of entrepreneurs.

6. Take part in competitions for young designers

Many games are organized for young entrepreneurs. Don't hesitate to participate; it's an excellent way to make yourself known! You will be spotted by the media, invited to trade fairs, shows... But be reactive because journalists are people in a hurry! You have to be able to respond quickly to their request.

7. Be very professional!

Your young age and, no doubt, your lack of professional experience must be compensated by the seriousness and professionalism you will prepare for your business project.

8. Go for it (a little ...)

Take the lead! Find the media that interest you, and that can help you depending on your activity. Locate the correct columnist and thump on their entryway. Try not to spare a moment to contact business people who could open their organization to you. Join clubs for business creators.

9. Don't be discouraged

It is challenging to be a business chief ... Starting a business requires a ton of time and energy. There will be good and bad times, some terrible news, and a touch of exhaustion can demotivate you. Be that as it may, have faith in your venture, and don't surrender!

Know how to surround yourself with people (spouse, friends, family, associates, advisers, etc.) who believe in you and learn how to boost you in difficult times.

10. Know when to stop on time

A big part of the associations exists following five years, yet that doesn't suggest that there is a half dissatisfaction." Even failure is right, because starting a business is an experience that will allow you to bounce back. Even if it didn't work, having set up a business is a real plus in a CV. Entrepreneurship is a quality sought by recruiters. Discover some testimonials from young entrepreneurs without diplomas who have started!

Pros And Cons To Hiring Family Members

Why Trust Hop Interim To Recruit A Member Of Your Family?

As a business manager, you have the possibility of recruiting an acquaintance to respond to a peak in activity or replace an absent employee. In this case, two types of employment contracts are available to you: the fixed-term contract (CDD) or the temporary employment contract (CTT). Do you not know which one to choose? Follow the guide!

Being the leader of a business takes a lot of time and energy. And who says recruitment necessarily says administrative procedures with different organizations. This new task, which is added to your already busy schedule, you can entrust to us.

Our team takes care of the administrative management of the employment contract.

At Hop Interim, the principle is simple: you recruit the person of your choice (family member, relative, former interim) and take care of all the administrative parts related to the employment contract. For your part, all you have to do is provide us with information about your company and your employee.

You make significant financial savings, by hiring a family member yourself, you save on sourcing and recruiting costs charged by an employment agency. And this is not negligible, especially if you are a tiny business leader or an SME. Thanks to Hop Interim, an interim that you pay at the minimum wage. By way of comparison, in a classic acting agency.

You comply with the legislation on temporary work, In the Labor Code, there are many measures concerning the hiring of a temporary employee. For a business manager, it is challenging to know all the specifics of each employment contract. By using Hop Interim, you make sure you are complying with the law. Our team is regularly trained in temporary employment legislation and can call on competent services if necessary.

You fight against remote work. As a business owner, it may seem simple to recruit a member of his family without having him sign a fixed-term contract or an interim contract. But be aware that this is not legal and that in the event of an inspection, you risk a lot, mainly because you will be accused of using remote work (or moonlighting).

Finally, when you hire an acquaintance on an interim contract, they are protected like any other employee and benefit from the social benefits linked to their agreement: remuneration, bonuses if applicable, end of mission indemnities (IFM), compensatory leave indemnities. Paid (ICCP), Right to unemployment.

Pros And Cons Of Hiring Family Members

It stays in the family. But do these truths hold in the workplace? Working with your family can have a lot of benefits. It is always said that blood ties are the strongest. Family first. It stays in the family. But do these truths hold in the workplace? Working with your family can have a lot of advantages, but indeed there are some disadvantages. We'll take a look at it.

BENEFITS:

- **It's about your family** - you know them, and they know you: Something is reassuring about you that you don't have to sell yourself to anyone. Working with family can save you time and reduce stress in this regard. Your family probably knows your strengths and weaknesses, and vice versa. With this knowledge already in place, you can move forward and develop your business plan faster, and we say move on because you don't waste time in the preliminary stages.

- **You like them, and they like you (we hope!):** While appreciating the people you work with isn't always considered essential, we believe it is necessary, especially when you venture out and start your own business. As a family, assuming you like each other, the absence of hate will create a much happier and more productive work environment. Also, there is the belief that when working alongside someone whom you admire and love, the possibilities to do better and, therefore, to be successful are higher.

- **Familiarity and Camaraderie Fit In:** As mentioned above, a positive work environment is often linked to higher productivity. Working with someone whose company you enjoy, who shares interests with you, and who you can joke with really helps maintain that supportive environment.

- **Trust:** The circle of trust doesn't need to develop, which can be exceptionally comforting for many people. Your group of friends stays small, and it's possible to have more candid conversations around family members because you trust them. Families tend to stick together. You don't have to survey the field and design tests for family members because trust is just innate.

DISADVANTAGES:

- **Discipline:** Disciplining employees is never easy, and it could get even more complicated with someone as close to you as a family member. These kinds of situations can be very embarrassing and painful and can lead to family conflicts.

- **Rules:** Some family members may find it challenging to obey rules set by a sibling or parent. They may feel that they are above these "mundane" rules because, after all, they are family! This idea that the restrictions don't apply can lead to unpleasant work habits and disrupt the workplace.

- **Separate the link from work:** Since your family is your family first and foremost, it can be challenging to classify this at work. Switching every moment from title to nickname doesn't have to be straightforward. Because of this difficulty in making this distinction, family members may find it challenging to understand their role. Also, it can lead to inappropriate behavior or treatment due to false expectations.

- **Resentment:** If something wrong happens or one member is more successful than the other, it may arouse some resentment. While not deliberate, this resentment can have lasting effects on family relationships and a ripple effect on the whole family.

Don't Celebrate Without Paying Taxes.

So you are getting an assessment discount, and it feels very generous. Should you not be celebrating? All a tax refund means is the government has had an interest-free loan from you, and can you afford to do that? I can't.

That isn't discovered cash; however, if you are getting an expense discount, here are a couple of approaches to put the money to utilize:

» Increase your retirement savings, helping you to secure a promising future while reducing your tax bill next year is a win/win.

» On the off chance that you have kids, perhaps the best speculation you can make in their future is via post-optional instruction. Consider putting that money into an RESP.

» None of us knows for sure when the roof will leak or find yourself unemployed If you don't have a backup stash, start one with your discount. Some state has enough cash to cover three months. Worth of living expenses. I recommend a half year or perhaps a year. Err on the side of caution.

- » Give to your favorite charity and reap the benefits of having a significant tax deduction while enjoying the use of giving back.
- » Consider replacing old appliances that are no longer energy efficient. A newer model could wind up saving you money.
- » Make yourself more marketable by using the refund to take additional courses, so you remain current and competitive.
- » Thinking of a short-term purchase like a home?
- » Save the refund and put it into a Tax-Free Savings Account.

Importance Of A Good Cpa

Do you ever feel the need for an accountant? Assuming no, at that point, trust me, you're not mindful of their significance. Accountants are a boon for the business owners. It won't be wrong to call them the backbone of financial management. However, they are no counterpart for confirmed public accountant

A certified public accountant is a more qualified version of an accountant who will manage your finances, audit your taxes, and perform other essential functions. As an entrepreneur, you have to zero in on a few business offices at the same time.

However, the accountant's office is a significant one that requests complete consideration. Wouldn't it be smarter to employ a specialist to deal with your records office? In such cases, you can generally hire a CPA. He will keep you educated about changing assessment laws, set up your budget summaries, and so forth.

You might perceive it as an additional expenditure. Instead, he will turnaround your business by keeping your finances in order. It's in every case, better to realize a CPA's significance before recruiting one! When you get to know jobs, you would not desire to defer in employing an effective public affirmed bookkeeper.

9 Important Qualities Of A Great Accountant

In case you're looking for an Accountant for your business, you presumably have a rundown of boxes you need to be ticked to guarantee you're getting the best experts accessible. Of course, every business owner wants qualities like:

- » Highly organized
- » Attentive to detail
- » Manages time well
- » Adaptable
- » Communicates articulately
- » Works hard
- » Learns easily
- » Creative
- » Trustworthy

In any case, those are characteristics you'd anticipate from almost everybody you work with, correct? At Scrubbed, we like to think there are different characteristics your accountant ought to have that are more specific to the finance industry and help guarantee your business's success.

These characteristics aren't just related to one person but should be embraced company-wide.

Here's our list of the nine top qualities of a significant accounting firm to help you find the pros who are best suited for your business:

POSSESSES DIVERSE KNOWLEDGE

Accounting is more than just keeping a ledger by adding and subtracting numbers. There are many moving parts to account for, and sometimes startup entrepreneurs aren't even aware of all the elements encompassed by accounting. We think good accountants are often most helpful when they tell you what you don't already know, helping you find areas for financial improvement you never knew existed.

Your business accountants should have knowledge diversity to provide a broad range of services. You don't want to have to go to one accountant for your checkbook management and another for your taxes. Scoured is satisfied to offer administrations in the accompanying zones:

- **Accounting and bookkeeping:** general ledger maintenance, bank reconciliation, purchase-to-pay, order-to-cash, cost accounting, inventory system support, financial reporting, and payroll setup and support
- **Corporate finance:** financial modeling, pitch decks, transaction advisory services, and financial planning and analysis
- **Tax compliance and advisory:** tax planning, state and local taxes, tax support services, and income tax preparation and filing

- **Professional support:** SOX (Sarbanes-Oxley) compliance, audit support, controllers, and transaction advisory for buy-side and sell-side (mergers and acquisitions)

HAS SERIOUS EXPERIENCE

Being able to offer a sweeping array of services properly can only come from experience. You want to know that your accountants have performed these tasks many times. The best way to find out if an accountant is experienced in the areas you require is first to check out their website (they have

a website, don't they?) and then ask about specifics in your initial consultation. Any accountants you consider should have testimonials or be able to offer references from previous or ongoing clients.

It could be enticing to go with a bookkeeping firm of more established workers, thinking they'll have the experience you need. But while you don't want a firm of only recent graduates, there's no guarantee senior accountants have the expertise you require. Some near-retirement accountants may have practiced law or real estate first, or spent more time managing than performing actual accounting tasks. A generally youthful firm with aggregate long periods of involvement frequently gives you a ton of active foundation information with the energy to take care of business for you.

WORKS WITH YOUR BUSINESS SECTOR

Your accountant information and experience ought to reach out to your specific zone of business. While ideally, a prospective accounting firm will have dealt with many different types of industry, they need to have worked with yours. A bookkeeper who just handles car shops, for instance, won't almost certainly be comfortable with the subtleties of representing a cannabis business.

Make sure to ask any accountant you are meeting on the off chance they have your business type. Assume you need a strength bookkeeper for a specialty business. In that case, it's more important that they have experience specific to your area than to find an accountant that's handled thousands of clients but none close to your business.

STAYS ON TOP OF INDUSTRY CHANGES

Connected at the hip with an accountant that comprehends your business area is their capacity to remain current with industry changes. Naturally, you'll anticipate that your accountant should think about new expense codes and account law that influences your endeavor. Yet, you additionally need them to think about patterns in your industry, similar to business measurements, compensations, re- appropriating, significant new enactment, and late consolidations and acquisitions.

UNDERSTANDS THE RANGE OF BUSINESS SIZES

Have you moved toward accountant already, just to discover they arrange with massive global aggregates? Conversely, have you seen some firms don't understand the complexity of anything larger than a small office?

Your bookkeepers should be OK with a scope of business sizes. Why? So they can change and grow with you. You don't want to switch the accountant's midstream if a sudden influx of cash boosts you out of startup territory.

Nor would you like to surrender your present bookkeepers if, as a massive organization, you turn off another business as a startup adventure.

Alongside understanding diverse business sizes is being alright with different unfamiliar business settings and markets. For instance, Scrubbed has workplaces in San Francisco and the Philippines, which gives them an edge by being comfortable with both Asian and American business conditions.

USES LATEST TECHNOLOGY

It's incredible for your accountant to have the most assorted foundation conceivable and one that adjusts impeccably with your business. It's far superior if they can apply the most recent innovation to make your bookkeeping rehearses more proficient. Not only will you save money in the long run, but you'll also know there are fewer errors, and you'll be able to stay abreast of your industry and your competition.

At Scrubbed, we use the top programming stages and ability to incorporate these with your IT and momentum strategic approaches for the most consistent bookkeeping accessible. A portion of the top projects and steps we use include:

- Zero
- Expensify
- Gusto
- Dear Systems
- Bill.com
- Cin7
- QuickBooks

Tablets handle all the functions listed above and more. We make it our objective that on the off chance that you need a bookkeeping administration, we'll give it and do it well.

MAINTAINS PROPER CERTIFICATIONS AND CONTINUING EDUCATION

To have the option to offer the most recent innovation to our Scrubbed customers, we take keeping up all the correct accreditations and going through proceeding with schooling genuinely. That this is something you should request from any bookkeeping firm you are thinking about working with.

At Scrubbed, we maintain unique relationships with the accounting programs and platforms we use for our clients. Our staff goes the additional mile to get confirmed in the projects they're utilizing, and our volume of involvement guarantees our customers we realize how to get the most from these services:

- Zero: Platinum Champion Partner
- Expensify: Approved Bronze Partner
- Gusto: Silver Partner
- Dear Systems: Proud Partner
- Bill.com: Guru
- Cin7: Proud Partner
- QuickBooks: Certified QuickBooks User

When you work with Scrubbed, you can rest assured that only knowledgeable staff about these platforms are doing with your books.

HAS SECURITY AND INTERNAL CONTROLS

If you're giving your accountants all your financial information and perhaps even access to your inventory systems, checkbook, and tax filing, you want to ensure your data stays secure.

Here are some wellbeing estimates that bookkeepers like Scrubbed use to ensure your business isn't in danger of security penetrate, regardless of whether through digital burglary or human blunder:

-Group pioneer with subtasks isolated among faculty as methods for inside control by restricting admittance to an excess of monetary data

- » Updated hardware and latest software, whether internal or SaaS (software as a service using a subscription plan, often cloud-based)
- » Password protection and cybersecurity measures, including data encryption
- » Employee screening and vetting
- » Employee certification on relevant software
- » Backup plan for data in the event of a natural disaster or other disruption

MAKES WORKING TOGETHER EASY

At long last, collaborating with your bookkeepers should be a delight, not a migraine. Keep in mind and they are working for you, not the reverse way around.

- » Here are a few signs that a bookkeeping firm is client-driven:
- » At your initial meeting, they ask many questions about your business, rather than merely providing information about themselves.

» They offer administrations that develop with you, with a scope of value levels that consider specific size businesses at different phases of improvement.

» The accountant offers staffing consistency rather than

» a rotating entryway of experts each time you meet.

» They have time for your calls and respond promptly to questions or requests you have.

» They treat private companies and huge partnerships similarly well. While doing your books, making arrangements for a review, or helping you prep for a significant speculator's meeting, they disclose the cycle to you.

» They offer proactive strategies at regular intervals and don't just provide the bare minimum at urgent deadlines.

» Instead of adding to your bill, they show you how

» you can set aside cash with your bookkeeping firm.

Learn To Outsource Or To Delegate Workloads, You Can't Do It Alone

How To Succeed In Outsourcing In Business?

When you have just created your business, you often want to do everything simultaneously. However, a good business organization necessarily passes at one time or another through partial subcontracting.

Yes, but how do you succeed in business outsourcing?

If you don't yet know what this means or how to delegate, this article is for you! Let's see to what extent entrusting specific missions to third parties can be beneficial.

Outsourcing: definition

Are you a new entrepreneur? May you not have heard of the word "outsource" yet? No worries, let's see its explanation together. Behind that word hides a compelling concept that can help you increase your sales while making your life easier.

Outsourcing means having recourse to another person to relieve the management of part of your activity.

At first glance, this term can sometimes scare entrepreneurs, yet its implementation is relatively simple and offers many advantages for improving its business.

Once the theory is exposed, you now wonder how to succeed in outsourcing in business? By what means, who to recruit, when to decide, I tell you everything on the subject, so that you, in turn, derive all the benefits!

If you are recruiting for the first time, I invite you to read my complete file to accompany you step by step!

Why outsource part of your activity?

The first answer is: saving time, of course. It is the most invaluable resource we have.

Much more precious than money if you lose money, you can find more. When you lose time, you never get it back. The execution of administrative or accounting formalities is an exceptionally time-consuming task.

Although they are essential to perform, in reality, few people enjoy taking care of them. Worse, many of us don't have the skills. It will then be necessary to understand how to achieve them. T represents an even greater waste of time, not to mention the risk of making mistakes if the way things are done is not right.

Entrusting your bookkeeping to a third party takes this weight off your shoulders and avoids unnecessary headaches. Some people have the skills to do these operations and will do it quickly. During this time, you can take care of areas that interest you more, on which you know, and with higher added value.

That outsourcing allows you to focus on what will make your company progress in the market and win new customers, for example. By focusing on what matters to move your business forward, your bottom line will be positively impacted. Finally, it is about knowing how to establish priorities.

> » What you can do,
>
> » What you can do,
>
> » What you want to achieve to grow your business.

How To Outsource And Delegate Specific Tasks Within Your Company

Knowing how to outsource and delegate tasks within your company are recommended because it becomes challenging to manage everything alone over time and with the loads. Therefore, it is essential not to experience stress and overwork to delegate and outsource specific simple or more complicated tasks within your company. Thus, it is necessary to follow several efficient steps or parameters to get the jobs done in the best possible way.

HOW TO OUTSOURCE SPECIFIC TASKS

An outsourcing contract is generally for a period of around 3, 5, or even seven years. Unlike a subcontract, in an outsourcing contract, the logic of partnership prevails. Indeed, the service quality here is more than essential, and the economic criterion is just secondary.

Thus, services such as reception, IT, logistics, or even payroll to specialized and private providers. The results are critical elements for successfully outsourcing specific tasks.

However, there are many steps to follow for successful outsourcing. Already, we must identify the strategic functions. That means determining the needs of the business before choosing the task to outsource.

Then, you should take good care of your company's internal communication to avoid worrying employees. This step can be long depending on the companies and employees. Establish specifications that must include many essential points, such as a complete description of the entire function to be outsourced, its role for the company, and its necessary material and human resources. A reversibility clause that contractualises the exit conditions at the end of the contract must be included.

Other criteria must also be considered (finance, service provider specifications, visit premises, and many others). Once you have made your decision, all that remains is to organize the transfer and ensure the follow-up of services.

HOW TO DELEGATE SPECIFIC TASKS WITHIN YOUR COMPANY

To succeed in delegating tasks in a company with precision and ease, it is like with outsourcing to follow steps.

First, be patient and give your partner time to understand your methodology on an excellent delegation process. Know which tasks to delegate, because even if some studies seem easy to charge, you will remain responsible for that task.

Surround yourself with the right people to reassure you of their competence, professionalism, trust, and loyalty. Thus, you will delegate tasks to members of your team who have the required skills.

Provide details on why you are delegating these tasks. Why did you choose this or that resource to charge, how it will help you, etc? We should be precise and communicate better to waste less time. Be clear and say what you expect clearly that that will allow for a job well done.

You Can't Do It All Alone.

The problem is, you are only human, like all of us. You only have 7-8 hours of work in your day, no more and no less, and you won't be able to do everything on your own.

And that is not to mention that after 4 hours of work in full concentration mode, your brain will tire and will only be good at dealing with less complex tasks requiring less concentration. For example, send an email.

Duplicate And Scale-Up

DEFINITION OF DUPLICATION

Duplication is the ability to reproduce something of value reliably. Replication allows you to make copies of your offer quickly and inexpensively, making it more widely available in a cost-effective way. To make something that doesn't need your immediate contribution, you should have the option to copy adequately.

DEFINITION OF SCALE-UP

A scale-up is the point at which you foresee what will occur in a cycle as a result of things you have seen in a comparative, however more modest process. To scale up is characterized as to make something more terrific or bigger.

A significant scale-up of the atomization is refined if comparable bead sizes, bead speeds, and splash densities are accomplished in the creation scale as in the research facility scale.

A reliable scale-up of a cycle condition from a model to full-scale must be accomplished if the dimensional investigation managed the issue. A scale-up is the point at which you foresee what will occur in a cycle on account of things you have seen in a comparative yet more modest process.

How Do You Duplicate Yourself In A Business?

As a business owner, it's your job to create systems that deliver value to the marketplace.

Need Help to Grow Your Business Faster? Here are Four Ways to "Clone" Yourself

» Build a team around you.

» You will need to advertise.

» Sell digital assets.

» Automate.

The Power of Duplication: Scaling a Business up. One process at a time. Have you ever wanted for a clone of yourself to complete more in your business?

Have you ever thought to yourself that if you weren't facilitating the business affairs, would the company continue to thrive? Have you ever wanted to grow your business but did not know how you would without compiling a mountain of debt?

A solution to this dilemma is growing a business from the inside out by using duplication. The power of repetition is essentially focused on identifying and executing efficiencies within your business, and you can do it in five easy steps.

The first step is to view a business as a human body, with the industry's different segments representing body parts that have other functions and complete various processes. For your body parts to function correctly, there must be an efficient process in place for them. For example, when a person wants to walk, their brain will send the signal down to their legs, and the legs will respond.

However, if you have a broken or sprained ankle, your ankle cannot function properly, and neither can your leg. Your ankle knows what to do, but because your ankle is not working, the process of walking is broken.

That is the same way in a business – when there is a breakdown in the process, other parts of the company cannot function efficiently. Yet, some companies will go months or even years without making the proper changes until inefficiencies worsen and spread throughout the business.

In this manner, the primary critical advance in duplication is to sharpen the business measures. Like advertising, every business function, hiring employees, shipping, selling, producing, and invoicing, has a strategy behind it. It is incredibly vital to examine every business process and then provide easy yet detailed steps for all employees to understand and follow.

By providing concise instructions and actions, the business unit's internal structure can establish better protocols and increase efficiency. While going through these steps, additional protocols can be put into place and set automation where possible. By automating processes, fewer mistakes are made, and the remaining errors can be easily traced to the source quickly. That is the next step – to automate the process.

Automation streamlines the process to be easily duplicated and makes the process more efficient. That will save time and money, which will increase profits. Many companies typically give up profit margins because their operations are not efficient and duplicable. A business has to take on some additional expenses to establish business processes, but investing in business processes will significantly benefit.

So, the third step is to invest in better methods. With the consistent cycles set up, any certified people should have the option to follow steps and execute.

After establishing these efficient processes, the fourth step is to hire more talented people to manage the operations. That is the "clone" everyone is looking for, and it allows managers and executives to focus on other aspects of the business.

By identifying motivated, experienced, and engaged individuals, a business owner or manager can create a team of like-minded individuals and elevate the industry.

Now that a company has the right processes with the right people, the fifth and last step is to sell the operation.

Most franchises are incredibly profitable because they have a process that can be duplicated, and people buy franchises for this very reason.

- These franchisees buy into a fair process, and this method can be used on a smaller scale for any company.
- By following the first four steps, a company has built a sellable product–efficient processes that improve a business. That can now be sold and taught to other companies who need their strategies revamped.

Pay Yourself

What It Means to Pay Yourself First

"Pay yourself first" means that you should pay your savings and investment accounts first. You are "paying" your future self by putting something aside for your drawn-out requirements and costs. For example, paying yourself can include:

- » Putting money into your retirement accounts
- » Buying insurance, including life insurance and long-term disability care
- » Paying into a health savings account
- » Creating an emergency fund
- » Paying off debts

At the point when you pay yourself first, you are organizing your drawn-out monetary prosperity. Instead of zeroing in just on immediate necessities, for example, bills or amusement, you pay your future self by sparing before you do some other spending.

How To Start Paying Yourself First

It can be daunting to start paying yourself first when you already feel like you struggle to keep up with your bills and other spending. Be that as it may, if you separate your objectives into sensible advances, it will be simpler to begin sparing. There is an assortment of approaches to do this.:

Automate Your Savings the money you get in a paycheck doesn't have to all go to the same place. If you make enough money but have trouble saving, automate it by sending your salary to different accounts.

You can have a specific measure of your salary saved into you're:

» Retirement accounts

» HSA

» Savings accounts

The money will never appear in your checking account, and you won't have to worry about spending it. You can also set up these transfers from your checking account; make sure you set them for the day after you are paid, not to have the opportunity to spend your savings on other things.

PAY OFF DEBT FIRST

For example, if you have a high-interest obligation, individual advances, or charge card obligation, center around taking care of that first.

Something else, the interest installments will keep on eating into your capacity to spare.

Utilizing either the torrential slide or snowball strategy, assign a specific measure of every check to take care of obligation. Make this installment quickly every time you are paid; that way, you won't chance to spend your obligation installment on different things.

Whenever you have dispensed with your obligation, take the cash you put towards installments and begin placing it into reserve funds and retirement accounts.

PAY IN ADVANCE

When you purchase life coverage or handicap protection, you can make regularly scheduled installments, or you can pay for the whole year on the double.

On the off chance that you need to pay yourself first, creating yearly installments can help.

5 Steps To Pay Yourself First And Grow Your Wealth

STEP #1:   RUN THE NUMBERS

To pay yourself first, you have to do the regularly feared errand of planning. Tweet this.

That doesn't mean you need to have detailed spreadsheets and annotated notes of each purchase you make – but it helps.

Record all your high costs in a month: lease, food, wireless bill, utilities, and transportation costs, credit installments, and so on". Throw in a 10 percent buffer to be safe. Then subtract this number from your monthly income.

For instance, Leslie procures $2,500 per month (after expenses and her 401(k) commitment). Leslie's bills and living expenses cost her $1,550 a month. She adds an extra

$250 cushion to her costs if something goes wrong. Leslie subtracts her living expenses and bills from her monthly income: $2,500 – $1,800 = $700.

STEP #2: SET A SUM TO SPARE EVERY MONTH

Proceeding to utilize Leslie, for instance, she has $700 staying in the wake of covering every one of her tabs and transportation expenses and purchasing goods.

Leslie chooses to give herself $100 per week to spend on shopping, amusement, or miscellaneous items she may need to purchase. Cleaves her with $300 every month in "squirm room."

Rather than leaving this cash in her ledger, Leslie makes an arrangement to naturally move $300 per month into reserve funds when she gets paid. Leslie gets paid two times per month, so she should contribute $150 of every check into a bank account."

STEP #3: SET UP A SAVINGS ACCOUNT WITH A DECENT INTEREST RATE

Checking accounts are not the appropriate place to be saving money. Why?

Since the loan fees on most financial records will procure you a penny a year. Even the savings accounts at many traditional banks are relatively lackluster. Instead of settling for a 0.01% interest rate, be sure to search around for the savings accounts with the highest interest rates.

Internet-only banks like Ally, Barclays, GE Capital Bank, and Synchrony Bank Optimizer+ offer rates of 0.90%and higher.

T might sound insignificant, but on $4,000 in savings, it's the difference between 40 cents in interest and $38 a year.

STEP #4: AUTOMATE SAVINGS

On the off chance that you can't believe yourself to pay yourself first, at that point, it's ideal for mechanizing reserve funds. Tweet that Thusly, the cash coming into your record will simply be the cash for charge paying and spending. You won't have to worry about the temptation to spend money you should be saving.

Checks paid through the direct store can undoubtedly be part of sending a rate into a bank account. Speak to your employer about deferring a set amount from each paycheck into a savings account. Or on the other hand, you can mechanize the exchange from your bank. Simply be sure you don't incidentally wind up in an overdraft circumstance since it mechanizes to set aside cash that isn't in your account yet.

STEP #5: ADJUST HOW MUCH YOU SAVE

Not everyone can be like Leslie and save $300 each month. You may run your numbers and realize you can only afford to keep $2 out of each paycheck. Don't be discouraged.

The critical part of paying yourself first is to take action. Tweet this: It is a lot simpler to fabricate the propensity for sparing ahead of schedule as opposed to getting into the penchant for going through the entirety of your cash and attempting to recalibrate further down the road."

If all you can afford for the first year is $2 a month, then still diligently save those $2 a month. Many online savings accounts don't have a minimum requirement for setting up an account, so you can feasibly save $2 a month without non-sufficient funds penalties.

As your income increases (or debt decreases), then adjust how much you defer into savings.

Anthony Robinson

Keep Personal Accounts And Business Accounts Separate.

WHAT IS THE DEFINITION OF A PERSONAL ACCOUNT?

The distinction is made between individual statements and other banking and accounting charges because different account types have different implications and treatments. There are probably many users in a business account extracted from a large pool of money to run a business.

For an individual record, there should just be one individual saving and pulling out cash. In this manner, safety efforts will be set up to ensure the suitable individual is getting to the assets. Personal accounts are often kept completely separate from business and joint accounts because they are entirely in one user's interest rather than many.

WHAT IS A BUSINESS ACCOUNT?

Business accounts are utilized to follow the money balance, cash owed to the business, cash owed to banks, and finance paid to representatives. The number of records a business needs will differ. However, business accounts are general to all organizations.

A business needs a framework to deal with its cash. Business accounts are used to track the cash balance, money owed to the company, money owed to creditors, and payroll paid to employees. The number of accounts a business needs will vary, but business accounts are universal for all businesses.

How To Separate Business And Personal Finances

- » To have the option to outline business and individual exchanges, there are a couple of steps you have to count on before you head: Register and join your business (on the off chance that you haven't as of now) T includes applying for an Employer Identification Number, which you'll use on tax returns, applications, and other financial documents and accounts.

- » Determine how to pay yourself. It's not as simple as just depositing the funds you receive from customers into your bank accounts; you need to set up a calculated system.

- » Open your business financial accounts. That includes a checking account and a credit card. You may likewise need to consider a business investment account.

- » Apply for a business credit card. Even if you don't use it, this will give you a credit history that you can lean on in your later stages.

- » Sign up for accounting software and link your financial accounts. Track income and expenses for your business here.

- » Reason Why You Should Keep Your Business and Personal Bank Accounts Separate

Organized Bookkeeping

Using your credit card or debit card for business expenses makes it challenging to distinguish between business and personal transactions on your bank statement.

Setting up a different financial balance lets you effectively track your business exchanges so you can:

- » Keep your bookkeeping accurate and up to date.

- » Try not to filter through long periods of explanations and receipts to isolate your business and individual costs come charge time.

- » Get caught up on year-end bookkeeping faster.

You can even associate your business financial balances to bookkeeping programming like QuickBooks or zero to continuously record your income and costs.

EFFICIENT TAX RETURNS

Keeping up isolated business and individual ledgers won't only spare you time during charge season. It will assist you in documenting more precise assessment forms.

Experiencing each line on your bank proclamations when business and individual costs are blended can take hours or even days and expand the opportunity you'll incorporate or reject the wrong items.

Utilizing separate records smoothed out your record-keeping by making it simple to distinguish available advantages and allowances.

Fun certainty: Did you realize the bank charges brought about to work your business or cycle instalments qualify as assessment deductible operational expense?"

CLEAR AUDIT TRAIL

One of the disadvantages is that you're bound to get evaluated.

The primary explanation entrepreneurs raise more warnings than individuals who work for another person is that worker T4 slips show a yearly profit, derivations, and duties withheld.

Utilizing a different financial balance won't ensure fewer reviews. But separating your business transactions and providing a clear audit trail will make the process less painful.

ACCURATE CASH FLOW MANAGEMENT

While your bank balance is by no means the complete picture of your cash flow, separating business and personal finances makes it easier to manage and react to your current cash situation.

For instance, if you notice that your equilibrium is coming up short, you can play out a fast money infusion. If you see there's too much money lying dormant in your account, you can put it to better use elsewhere.

"It's additionally simpler to exhibit your financial position when you keep up isolated business and individual financial balances. The more clear your financial records, the more straightforward it is to apply for subsidizing from a loan specialist or credit supplier.

BUSINESS CREDIBILITY AND PROFESSIONALISM

Whether you run a counseling firm or café, keeping up business believability is fundamental. While numerous entrepreneurs achieve this by making marked logos, sites, and advertising materials, keeping your business and individual records separate is another approach to show polished methodology."

Utilizing a business financial balance to make and get installments straightforwardly through your business sets up a more prominent degree of trust with providers and customers.

BUSINESS CREDIT SCORE

Utilizing a different business account helps fabricate your business FICO assessment. Similar to your credit rating, your business credit score is a reflection of your company's creditworthiness.

A reliable financial assessment can help you make sure about better terms for business credits and decrease business protection expense.

At Enkel, we encourage every one of our customers to keep separate business and individual ledgers. While our group centers on smoothing out your accounting and conveying detailed budget summaries, you can zero in developing your business. Reach us to become familiar with how we can assist you with keeping your books coordinated.

Don't Allow Your Good Heart To Create Bad Business Decisions.

12 REASONS YOU SHOULD NEVER REGRET ANY DECISION YOU EVER MAKE

1. **Every decision will enable you to take credit for creating your own life. Decisions are not always the result of thoughtful contemplation. Some of them are made without really thinking alone. Regardless of the decision, when you made it, it was something you wanted, or you would not have done it (unless someone was pointing a gun at your head).**

   Be willing to own the decisions you make. Be accountable for them. Take responsibility and accept them.

2. **By settling on any choice, including your heart, you get the opportunity to make more cherish on the planet by spreading yours." Your love is a gift.**

Once you decide to love, do it without reservation. By entirely giving of yourself, you expand your ability to express and receive love. You have added to the goodness of our universe by revealing your heart to it.

3. **By encountering the failure that may accompany a choice's result, you can push yourself to another degree of enthusiastic advancement."**

   You aren't doing yourself any favors when you try to save yourself from disappointment.

   Dissatisfaction furnishes you with an occasion to rethink your encounters throughout everyday life. By refining your reexamining abilities, you increment your strength.

4. **"Terrible" choices are your occasion to dominate the specialty of self-absolution.**

   At the point when you make an "awful" choice, you are the individual who is typically the hardest on yourself. Before you can accept the consequences of your decision and move on, you must forgive yourself.

   You won't generally settle on ideal decisions in your day-to-day existence. Recognize the excellence in your human defect; at that point, push ahead and on

5. **Because of the occasional misstep, you enable yourself to live a Technicolor life. Anger. Joy. Sadness. These emotions add pigment to your life. Without these things, you would feel soulless. Your life would be black and white.**

   Make your decisions with gusto. Breathe with fire.

   You are here to live in color.

An Introduction To Entrepreneurship

6. **Your capacity to settle on a choice is an occasion to practice the opportunity that is your inheritance.**

    How might you feel on the off chance that you had nothing to do with those choices concerning your life? OK, feel weak? Confined? Choked? Presently, the center around what it seems like to".

    Make the decisions you want to make. What do you think? Freedom? Liberty? Independence?

    What feelings do you want to feel? Freedom. Liberty. Independence.

    Coincidentally, the open door you need is yours.

    Be appreciative of it in each choice you make "great" or "terrible."

7. **When you make a decision resulting in ugly aftermath, you refine what you do want in your life.**

    It's regularly unrealistic to understand what you do need until you experience what you don't need. With every decision, you will experience consequences. Utilize those results as a hopping off highlight something else (and better) in your future.

8. **By feeling the torment from a choice "turned out badly," you empower yourself to relax in the radiance of choice "gone right."**

    "You won't know light without lack of definition, love without torment, nor mental spine unafraid. When you are experiencing something unwanted, embrace it. That circumstance, individual, or thing will permit you to perceive (and cherish) the brightness of that which you want when it turns into yours.

9. **For each "fizzled" choice, you will make an "effective" choice.**

   Even if you don't hit the mark every time, by continuing to make decisions, you realize several of your life's purposes: to experience, to learn, and to feel. Albeit not all choices work out. When they do, there isn't anything more refreshing.

   When they do, there is nothing more life-affirming.

   Furthermore, when you experience this satisfaction, you are propelled to move towards a more generous amount of what you hunger for.

10. **You will make no mistakes. You only will have experiences.**

    Begin contemplating "awful" choices as learning openings. Dependent on how you choose to figure, you will have the option to see that every decision holds regard. This overhauling will prompt various musings and convictions.

    When you start believing differently, your world will unfold differently; how this unfolding manifest is your choice.

11. **"Awful" results permit you to see that you are not your choices. Your choices don't characterize you as a "great" or a "terrible" individual. Your preferences help you remember the wisdom ever-present within your own heart. The consequences of your choices can fill in as a memorable reminder of what your identity is: divine flawlessness.**

12. Contingent upon how you decide to figure, you will have the option to see that each choice holds esteem.

There is a blessing in each choice you have ever constructed. With a shift in thinking, you will come to understand those gifts. You should simply ask yourself, "What is the blessing in this?" "And then check out your heart talk.

Conclusion

Being a business person requires assuming critical liability and accompanies enormous difficulties and expected prizes. The inspirations for turning into a business visionary are different. They can incorporate the potential for monetary pay, the quest for individual qualities and interests, and the premium in social change.

Summary

Entrepreneurship is tough to define. More specifically, the concept of entrepreneurship considers the impact on the environment and the influence of this environment to arouse business development by providing more or less vital resources and conventions.

Despite this, a narrow list of ten attributes suffices to characterize the entrepreneurial mindset on an operational level. The entrepreneur knows how to use his creativity to put it at the service of a vision, a personal objective, or a cause of the character of the entrepreneur.

An entrepreneur is a person who creates a project from a vision and resources in his possession. The basis of entrepreneurship that is the pillar that allows you to set a clear goal and guide your choices and actions towards this goal. Before you leave on the formation of a business, study your monetary circumstance well. You probably will not be able to pay yourself the first year of production. On the off chance that you live with your folks, it is ideal to remain there somewhat more!

www.ingramcontent.com/pod-product-compliance
Lightning Source LLC
Chambersburg PA
CBHW070828220526
45466CB00002B/782